Blogger's Quick Guide

to Writing Rituals and Routines

By Rebecca Livermore
Professional Content Creation
Littleton, Colorado

ISBN-13: 978-0692256169
ISBN-10: 069226164

DEDICATION

This book is dedicated to my husband, Chuck, for always believing in me.

CONTENTS

CONTENTS (CONT.)

A NOTE ABOUT MY BLOGGER'S QUICK GUIDE SERIES

I'm busy. You're busy. We're all busy. And when I polled my email list to find out what my audience wanted, the overwhelming response was in favor of short pieces that are very focused on a specific topic. That feedback is what inspired me to write a series of shorter books, and from there, my Blogger's Quick Guide series was born!

All of my blogging-related books that are on the shorter side (10,000 words or less) will have "Blogger's Quick Guide" on the cover and look similar to this book, so if you're looking for a quick read, these are the ones you'll want to go for.

Each of my *Blogger's Quick Guides* should be able to be read in about an hour, though, of course, reading speed varies person by person.

Also, while these books can be read fast, each chapter concludes with an optional writing prompt to help you internalize what you read. Whether you zip through each book fast, or take the time to write about what you read after reading each chapter is totally up to you.

WAIT! BECAUSE YOU ROCK!

Have you tried blogging consistently, only to find your blog languishing from lack of consistent blog posts?

I get it. Really.

I used to be the worst blogger ever. I started and abandoned multiple blogs. I just couldn't get into blogging consistently, regardless of what I tried.

That all changed two years ago, when I discovered the secrets to creating content consistently. I now make a comfortable, full-time living blogging.

MY GIFT TO YOU

As a thank you for purchasing this book, I want to give you my eCourse, *The Five Secrets to Developing the Blogging Habit*, absolutely free!

To get your complimentary eCourse delivered right to your inbox, go to:

www.professionalcontentcreation.com/blogginghabit.

CHAPTER 1
THE POWER OF BLOGGING RITUALS

A lot of people think of something mystical when they hear the words, "blogging ritual." For instance, they may think of something like burning incense, candles, Gregorian chants, meditation, and other mystical things.

But when I write about blogging rituals, that's not what I mean, although if burning candles or incense or doing other "mystical" things works for you, they can certainly be a part of your blogging ritual!

Let me let you in on a little secret: "ritual" is a more sexy sounding word for "routine." In fact, your blogging rituals can be no frills, and may even be considered boring by someone else, and yet be very effective for you.

The bottom line is that at least when it comes to blogging, the word, "ritual," and the word, "routine" can be used interchangeably, so what you call them doesn't matter.

The thing that will make a difference is actually making rituals and routines part of your blogging process in order to increase your blogging enjoyment and productivity.

Here are a few of the benefits of putting into practice the various blogging rituals and routines that I write about in this book.

1. Blogging rituals will help you get into the groove and beat writer's block.

As an example, if you do a certain action, such as brewing a particular tea blend, or sharpening pencils, or doing some stretching exercises immediately before you start to blog, whenever you start doing those actions in preparation for blogging, your mind and heart will immediately transition into blogging mode before you even turn on your computer!

2. Blogging rituals provide a sense of being in control.

Routines are the exact opposite of randomness and a lack of stability. Rather than allowing life and circumstances to dictate your behavior, rituals put you in the driver's seat as you take control over the blogging process.

3. Blogging rituals reduce anxiety.

Have you ever noticed that children thrive with routines? The reason is that routines naturally reduce anxiety because they let you know exactly what to expect. This reduced anxiety is a natural outcome of the two previous benefits of being in control, and overcoming writer's block. If you have good blogging rituals in place, you won't be filled with anxiety when you sit down to write.

4. Blogging rituals get rid of mental clutter and free your mind to write.

Mental clutter is a huge hindrance to getting things done, because it can paralyze you, and it certainly hinders your blogging productivity. When you have a blogging routine in place, you don't have to think as much about what you're going to do, and you'll be less likely to encounter roadblocks to getting your blog posts written.

5. Blogging routines expedite your entire writing process.

As I wrote earlier, blogging rituals make it easier to get into the writing groove. In addition to that, they tend to set off an entire process of routines that last beyond the actual ritual. For instance, not only will you start the writing process faster, with less procrastination, the sense of order present in the ritual will often spill over into the rest of the writing process.

When you consistently use the same routines, your entire writing process becomes more automatic. This order and automation reduces the amount of time you might waste with a more haphazard approach to your blogging.

Writing Prompt

Write about any writing rituals you've ever used. If you have never used any, jot down your thoughts about the process and how you feel about it, whether those thoughts are positive or negative.

CHAPTER 2
CLEAN UP YOUR OFFICE

Are you a blogger with a messy desk? Many bloggers are creative types, and not all, but many creative types are a bit, messy. Some, of course, are messier than others.

Other bloggers are outwardly neat and tidy, but have messes stuffed in closets and drawers.

Regardless of whether you're a closet messy, or a certified messy extraordinaire, or even if you're somewhat of a neat freak, a lack of organization can keep you from being a productive blogger.

Not only can it result in you wasting time looking for things that you need, it can even zap you of creativity, so that when you do sit down to write, the writing doesn't flow as well as it could.

Here are some things bloggers can do to clean up their work environment.

1. Remove all unnecessary items from the top of your desk.

Only you can determine what really needs to go on your desk. For instance, you may want family pictures on your desk, and maybe a couple of knickknacks. But the less clutter you have on your desk, the better.

I currently have just my computer monitor, a container with pens, and a small notepad on my desk. Obviously, while I'm working I may have some papers that I've printed off, and a book or two that I'm using for research, but for the most part, I keep my desk free of clutter. (And let me make a confession here: I'm a naturally messy person, so I have to work at this!)

The key is to tidy up your desk either at the start or end of each day, so that you always start each day with a neat work environment.

2. Organize your drawers and files.

If you've just tossed things like receipts, manuals, random papers and other items in your desk drawers, you'll waste a lot of time trying to find things when you need them. And while having the top of your desk tidied up is a good start, you need to take it a step further and clean up the hidden parts of your office that no one but you sees.

Clutter, even hidden clutter, can waste your time and make it harder to focus on the task at hand, blogging.

3. Clean up your computer files.

This may seem less important, especially since it's only a "virtual mess." But you can waste a lot of time trying to find documents and other items on your computer when everything is a mess.

The most important thing when it comes to computer filing is to have some type of a system that you use consistently.

I first learned the importance of this at one of my workplaces. A former employee had set up a computer filing system that everyone in my department used.

The value of this was that even if something had been filed by another person in my department, or even by someone who worked there several years before me, I could usually find a needed document in a matter of a few minutes.

If you have a ton of files that are a complete mess, create an archive folder and drag all files that are totally unorganized into that folder. They'll still be there if you need them, and getting them out of the way will help you start fresh.

Then set up a computer filing system for your business and everything related to your blog such as a system for organizing all of the blog posts you've written, the images you've downloaded, audio and video files, and so on.

4. Remove anything from your office that doesn't need to be there.

For some reason, random things that have nothing to do with work end up in offices. This is especially true if you work from home, since home life and blogging life, often intersect.

If an item that has nothing to do with your business has

somehow ended up in your office, get rid of it!

Obviously if you have a really messy work environment, it may take a good amount of time to get it cleaned up. If you don't have big chunks of time to devote to the cleanup, block out 30 minutes per day to work on cleaning up your office.

Focus on one small thing at a time, such as cleaning off your desktop, or one specific drawer or shelf. And whatever you do, don't let cleaning your office be an excuse to procrastinate when it comes to doing your actual blogging!

Make Tidying Up Your Office a Part of Your Routine

As I previously said, especially if you have messy tendencies like I do, even once you clean up your desk, it will get messy again. Because of this, it's good to make cleaning your desk part of your daily, or at the very least, weekly routine.

Writing Prompt

Have you found that having a clean work environment helps you be a more productive blogger, or do you think that messes enhance your creativity? Write about the clean/messy debate and the environment that best enhances your blogging.

CHAPTER 3
WRITE THE SAME TIME EVERY DAY

In an earlier chapter I wrote about writing rituals and routines, and how they can help you blog more consistently and be more productive in the time you spend blogging.

One of the routines that can help the most with your blogging consistency and productivity is writing the same time every day. This helps tremendously because being consistent in this way gets you into a mode that makes writing to be a more automatic and natural process, and as I'm sure you've experienced in other aspects of life, you won't have to work as hard on anything that has become automatic.

Night Owls Vs. Larks

For me personally, first thing in the morning is a must. I tried blogging other times during the day, but once my day gets started, other things dictate my priorities and before I know it, I'm sucked into one task after another until it's time to go to bed and I experienced yet another day without blogging. One "blogless" day leads to another until I've gone not just days, but weeks, without blogging.

The only way I've found to blog consistently is to do it first, before the demands of the day set in. This works for me because since I blog so early in the day, no one expects anything of me at that time. As far as everyone else is concerned, I may still be sleeping, so even seemingly pressing emails can be ignored until later, and unless there is a true emergency, no one calls me until later in the day.

Obviously, I'm a fan of getting up early, and it's pretty easy for me to do so because I'm naturally a morning person. *Now before you roll your eyes, and your defenses go sky high, let me assure you that I don't agree with the people who claim that EVERYONE should rise early.* The bottom line is that some people are more productive late at night, or perhaps early afternoon.

In fact, my husband really comes alive at midnight, and will often work on something all night long. While it's true that he can adapt and work "normal business hours," he's always been more productive at night. *The bottom line is that it's important for you to find a time that works best for you, and then be consistent* with it, so that it becomes even more natural to you.

For those who like more structure. . .

Now when I say to write the same time every day, I don't necessarily mean treating your blogging time as if you were punching a time clock. You don't have to write at the exact same time every day, though that type of rigidity definitely helps some people.

(As I wrote the previous words, I was reminded of a friend of mine who lived by a strict time schedule that she had written down and stuck to, down to the minute, as much as possible.

That would have stressed me out tremendously, but it seemed to work for her, and if you're so inclined, it can work for you as well!)

A common saying that I've heard is "What gets scheduled gets done" and many people advise putting the things that you're going to do on your calendar, for a specific time, and treating those things like any other appointment. Depending on the settings on your smart phone, if desired, you can even set it up so that you're reminded that it's time to blog!

So if you like a lot of structure, by all means, put your blogging time on your calendar, set up notifications on your phone that indicate that it's time to write, and sit down at exactly the specified time.

For those who prefer routines over schedules. . .

I've actually tried the super structured approach myself, but for whatever reason, that level of rigidity has never worked for me.

Instead of being rigid down to the minute, the thing that works for me is to write at approximately the same time every day, and rather than a precise time, write based on other set activities such as soon as I wake up. My goal may be to write starting at 5:00 a.m. every day, but some days I may sleep later and not start until 6:00. The key for me is to make writing one of the first things that I do each morning.

The bottom line with this less structured approach is to allow another activity to indicate that it's time to write. For instance, for me, it's simply after waking up in the morning. For a night owl, it may be after putting the kids to bed. For someone else, it may be after eating lunch or dropping the kids off at school. Find YOUR optimal time to blog and make that part of your daily routine.

Writing Prompt

In a perfect world, where you have complete control over your time, when is the best time for you to write? Are you more of a rigid, "punch the time clock" type of person, or are you more inclined to follow a routine that has approximate, but not set, times?

CHAPTER 4
HAVE A DAILY, WEEKLY, AND MONTHLY WORD COUNT GOAL

There are many ways to stay motivated as a blogger. One of the most common ways is to have a daily word count goal.

The concept is pretty simple, really: select a challenging but "doable" number of words that you will write each day, and then do it, EVERY day. The biggest problem with this approach is deciding how many words per day to commit to.

One way to figure this out is to start off with a daily time goal as written about in the next chapter, instead of a daily word count goal. For instance, determine to write at least 30 minutes per day. If you start off with writing a certain amount of time a day, track the number of words you write during that time. Do that for at least a month, and then that will give you a good idea of a realistic amount of words you can write daily.

Since every day is different, and there are other factors that figure into your ability to write a specific amount of words each day, I find it helpful to have a daily, weekly, and a monthly word count goal.

My daily goal of 500 words is pretty low. The reason I made

this decision is that 500 words is a low enough number of words that except under the most extreme circumstances, I can do it consistently.

Your daily word count goal may be even lower, such as 250 words. Part of the point of having a word count goal is to develop discipline and a habit, so if the goal is too high, you're almost setting yourself up for failure. Because of that, make sure to set a goal that you know you can reach consistently, with a moderate level of effort.

On the other hand, a goal that is too low isn't very motivating. After grappling with this, I found that a great way to have a low enough daily word count goal to make it doable, and yet to be appropriately challenging, was to also have a monthly word count goal that is much higher. I decided to make my monthly word count goal 20,000 words, which averages out to approximately 670 word per day (if I don't take weekends off). Because my monthly goal is as high as it is, I almost always push myself to write more than 500 words each day.

This balanced approach is what works for me, and you might want to give it a try yourself to see if it will also help you make progress when it comes to blogging consistently.

Writing Prompt

Have you had a daily word count goal? If so, what was your experience like with it? What was the most extreme writing goal you've ever had? If up to this point you haven't set any writing goals, what do you think you'll start with, a time goal, a word count goal, or a combination of the two? (You may need to read the next chapter before answering this question!)

CHAPTER 5
HAVE A DAILY TIME GOAL

In the previous chapter I wrote about having a daily word count goal as one way to boost your blogging productivity. That definitely works, and in fact is something that many bloggers do. When it comes right down to it, I hear about that one method of increasing writing output more than any other method.

There is another option, however, that you may want to try -- a daily time goal. This was my first, and for a long time, my favorite way to motivate myself to blog consistently.

A time goal is exactly what it sounds like -- blogging for a set amount of time each day. For example, setting a goal of blogging for 30 minutes per day, or an hour. I've even done it for 15 minutes with success.

In fact, my first daily time goal was to spend 15 minutes per day writing. I set that goal at a time when I felt that I didn't have much time to write, but knew that I needed to make writing a habit if I ever wanted to get anywhere with my writing.

The reason that this method works, even with a very short amount of time such as 15 minutes, is that anything when done consistently, will yield results -- even if the time is limited.

There are some advantages of having a daily blogging time goal instead of a daily word count goal. For one thing, time is something that you can control more than the number of words you write.

As an example, let's say that you're still working a day job, but you want to blog consistently, and the only (or best) time for you to do so is your lunch break at work. Since that is a limited window of time, and since sometimes words don't flow as quickly as you'd like, you could get into trouble if you had to push yourself to keep writing until you hit a certain number of words.

Obviously, this same problem could pop up even if you don't have a day job, but have other responsibilities, such as needing to get kids to school. It's definitely easier to schedule out a certain amount of time to blog than a certain number of words.

Even if you're not on a super rigid schedule such as someone with a day job, or a parent needing to get kids to school on time, you may like the simplicity of just setting a timer and writing for a certain length of time each day.

I especially recommend this if writing is a painful thing for you, and is something you really dread. Your attitude can be, "I can do ANYTHING for 15 minutes!" And once 15 minutes becomes easier for you, you can gradually increase the time.

All of those are positive reasons for having a time goal rather than a word count goal.

But there is at least one negative thing about having a time goal rather than a word count goal, and it's that you may not get much work done. With a set amount of time to blog each day, you could set your timer, and then end up day dreaming a big chunk of that time and still say that you wrote during that time.

In contrast, a word count goal demands that you produce a certain amount of volume each day, which can be a huge help when it comes to putting out a good volume of content.

What I would recommend is trying the time goal if you are a very scheduled person, and live by the things blocked out on your calendar in a very rigid way, or if your time to blog has to be fit in during specific time blocks such as lunch breaks.

If you find yourself slacking, and not getting much done in that time, then I'd recommend changing to a different method such as writing a set amount of words per day.

Writing Prompt

Having considered both a word count goal and a time goal, which one resonates with you the most? Taking that a bit further, if you plan to set a word count goal, how many words do you plan to write in a day, week, or month? If a time goal, how much time will you spend writing each day?

CHAPTER 6
GO ON A MONTHLY, QUARTERLY OR ANNUAL BLOGGING RETREAT

If you're the type of person that likes to focus on things in longer periods of time rather than trying to do something daily or weekly, having monthly, quarterly, or annual blogging retreats may be the way to go for you.

I personally think it would be really rough to write an entire year's worth of blog posts during a single retreat (even a long one!), but an annual writing retreat can still be helpful because even if you don't get an entire year's worth of posts written during that time, you can still make great progress and get ahead of the game. That can take the pressure off of you in times that you fail to meet your daily or weekly blogging goals.

If you go on a blogging retreat more frequently, such as monthly or quarterly, you may be able to make more progress on the actual writing during those more frequent retreats.

Here are a few ideas for writing retreats.

1. Start off by setting a primary goal for the retreat.

Ideally, you should set this goal before going on the retreat so you don't have to spend time during the retreat figuring out what you'd like to accomplish.

Be sure that your goal is challenging so that you'll be motivated to push yourself and get a lot done during your retreat, but keep it realistic so that the odds of it being a successful retreat are good. The bottom line is that you want to come away from your retreat with a sense of accomplishment.

2. Decide on a location for your writing retreat.

If you don't have the money to spend on heading to a hotel or a cabin in the woods, you can do a writing retreat at home, especially if you can be home alone.

Another alternative is to go to the library, or even a friend's home. If you opt to use a friend's home, it's best that she is away during the retreat unless the friend is going to participate in the retreat with you.

Obviously, it would have to be a very good friend to allow you to use her home when she is not there, but I've heard of this type of arrangement working well, and it's definitely worth considering if you don't have the funds to spend at a hotel or cabin.

3. Make sure you have everything you need -- and want -- for the retreat.

Even if you're having your blogging retreat at home, do some things to make it special. For instance, I love brewing my favorite tea to drink while I blog. Other practical things include your laptop, pen and paper, books you may need to research, an Internet connection, and so on. This will largely be up to you because it all depends on what will make you more comfortable and productive.

For example, while I mentioned an Internet connection in the previous paragraph, something you need may be a place that does NOT have an Internet connection! To decide what you really need for your blogging retreat, make a list of what you'd like to accomplish during the retreat, and everything you'll need to do what's needed.

Then, make a list of things that will make you more comfortable, and make the retreat more enjoyable for you. For instance, if your retreat is in the mountains, and you plan to do some walking, you'll want to make sure to pack hiking or comfortable walking shoes. If starting your day with coffee or tea is important, be sure to add those items to the list.

4. Reward yourself for a job well done.

If your blogging retreat lasts for more than a day, you may want to add in some pampering or fun during the retreat, to refresh and reward yourself. For instance, if you have a weekend retreat, on the afternoon of the second day, you may want to go for a massage, go hiking, or eat at a restaurant that would be a splurge for you.

Just do whatever it is that feeds your soul and makes you feel rewarded. You can have a bigger reward for accomplishing a more challenging goal.

If your retreat is shorter term, such as only a day, you probably won't want to use any of it on non-writing related items, but do plan to reward yourself at a later date if you are successful when it comes to meeting your goals for the retreat.

Writing Prompt

How do you feel about the idea of going on a writing retreat? Are you excited by the idea, or do you feel like you'd be bored to tears with concentrated times to write? Do you feel that you can realistically take the time for a retreat, or does the idea seem like a pipe dream?

CHAPTER 7
GO ON A WEEKLY ARTIST DATE

I first heard about artist dates in *The Artist's Way* by Julia Cameron. The basic idea of an artist date is to go on a weekly excursion that will help to nurture the artist in you. *There are few rules of artist dates, but one rule is that you must do them alone.* In other words, going on an artist date with a friend wouldn't be, according to Cameron, an artist date.

Now to be clear, artist dates don't have to be what many would consider to be "artistic." For example, they don't have to involve things like going to an art museum, or a shop where you make pottery, though they certainly could. The main idea is to do something that is fun and helps you refuel.

I first learned about artist dates when my kids were young, and for me they often included going out for coffee alone, with my journal. As a stay-at-home mom, getting out by myself once a week was a real treat, and definitely helped me refuel, but even if you aren't in a position of being around little kids all day every day, going on a weekly artist date can be immensely helpful in filling your tank so that the rest of the week, you find it easier to write.

Here are some artist date ideas. Feel free to use any -- or none -- of them, and of course feel free to come up with ideas of your own as well!

1. A coffee or tea date, with or without your journal. For me, the journal was a big part of my artist date.

2. Visit a nursery -- the kind with plants, not children. :)

3. Visit a bookstore and browse whatever looks interesting, rather than books that you "need" to read. Sometimes used bookstores are more fun since you never know what treasures you may find, but I also like stores with new books and good coffee, too!

4. Go on a nature walk. This doesn't have to be way out in the woods, though it can be. If you live in the city, find a nice park to take a walk in. Bring along a sketchbook, journal, camera, or all three!

5. Visit an art supply store. You don't necessarily need to buy anything, though you certainly can.

6. Go to a hobby shop. Hobby shops are similar to art supply stores, but often have other things that may inspire you such as rubber stamps, model kits, and who knows what else!

7. Do something to pamper yourself such as a massage, facial, or pedicure.

8. Go on a day trip to a nearby town and go exploring. Don't worry about having the whole day planned out, but instead, see what you can discover while there.

9. Take in a movie. Any type of movie is fine, but when it comes to my artist dates, I like ones that pull on my emotions.

10. Visit a gift shop, such as a Hallmark store, and browse through their collection of fun things that you don't really need. :) If you want to avoid spending money on something that will just clutter your home, leave your wallet in the car.

11. Bring a blanket to a park and do some cloud watching.

12. Write a letter to someone who means a lot to you. Unless you don't know how to contact them, mail the letter to them, and enjoy the fact that you'll be making their day when they receive it.

13. Browse an online shop such as Etsy, just for fun.

14. Have a picnic in the park. This doesn't have to be anything fancy, but if you have the time and energy to pack food you really enjoy, so much the better.

15. Go fishing. Try to go to a more isolated place if possible and while your focus will be on fishing, bring along a journal or other way to record your thoughts just in case you get some ideas to write about while you're waiting for the fish to bite.

16. Get out the art supplies and make something just for fun. If you have kids, use their silly things such as pipe cleaners and wiggly eyes to make something that you'd probably be embarrassed to show anyone!

17. Go to a museum gift shop. You can usually get into the gift shop free, and they often have really fun and creative items for sale.

18. Enjoy a meal at a cute cafe. Do some people watching while you're there! (I like to make up stories in my mind about the people around me to get my creative juices flowing.)

19. Visit a flower shop, and take time to smell the roses (and other flowers!).

20. Go to an ethnic grocery store and buy something you've never tried before. Go home and look for a recipe online using the ingredient and then cook an exotic meal.

21. Visit a planetarium. Enjoy the fact that you can take a trip to "space" without leaving earth. Let the wonder of space inspire you!

22. Go to a concert or live play. Relax and enjoy the performance, but make a point of also taking it all in in a much deeper way than you normally would. For instance, at a concert, pay close attention to the movement of the musicians, and the looks on their faces. Imagine what they may be feeling and thinking at the moment.

23. Go to a bus or train station or other busy place and people watch. Make up stories in your mind about the people there, and write about one of them.

24. Take a bath by candlelight. Have a good book to read and put on some relaxing music.

25. Go outside and yell something fun like, "Life I love you!" (This is a great one for a day when you don't have time for a "real" artist date!)

This list should get you started, but whether the items on this list appeal to you or not, make your own list as well. And remember that it's fine to do the same thing each week if that's what works for you. As a stay-at-home mom with little ones, my weekly coffee and journal dates were a great way to refuel and something I really looked forward to!

Writing Prompt

Write about all of the possible artist dates that you'd like to go on. Write about a dream one, even if it seems absolutely absurd, and then write about ones that you are 100% certain you can do.

CHAPTER 8
PUT ON YOUR WRITING CLOTHES

Some people swear by the importance of people who work from home getting dressed for work, meaning donning business attire, as if they were heading to a corporate job. For whatever reason, that's never worked for me, and in fact, the more comfortable I am, the better.

But since there truly are different strokes for different folks, I would experiment with different blogging attire to see whether or not it impacts your writing productivity. You can certainly give getting "dressed for work" a try to signal that it's time to sit down and write. Or like me, you may find that putting on something comfortable such as shorts or sweats is what does the trick.

I've heard it said that John Cheever, a Pulitzer Prize winning author wrote in his underwear most of the time. (If I tried that, with my luck, that's when the neighbors would drop by!)

You could have just one specific article of clothing such as a baseball cap, or a pair of slippers that you put on to signal that it's time to write.

The bottom line is that wearing the "right" thing when you write can make a difference in your writing productivity, so experiment a bit to find what works best for you!

Writing Prompt

Do you feel that what you wear impacts your ability to write? What writing "uniform" works best for you? What do you think of the guy who writes in his underwear? Is that something you'd do, or are you more of a business suit kind of writer?

CHAPTER 9
GO ON A MORNING WALK

A morning walk is a great way to kill multiple birds with one stone. First, if you are a full-time writer, or sit at a desk most of the day for any other reason, making a morning walk part of your daily ritual is a great way to get in some exercise, before the busyness of the day starts.

But walking is also a great way to get your creative juices flowing before you sit down to write -- even if you aren't able to get around to writing until later in the day.

While I mentioned exercise as a benefit of your morning walk, I've personally found it to be more beneficial (when it comes to increasing my creativity) to take a more leisurely stroll on a daily basis. In fact, I take my dog with me, and he makes a point of doing his best to slow me down, as he stops to smell the roses (and the not so rosy things!).

A huge benefit of making a morning walk part of your blogging routine is that sometimes the best way to break through writer's block is to get away from the computer.

The great news is that chances are, as you walk, you'll come up with multiple ideas for blog posts, so be sure to bring something with you to record those ideas. You could carry a small notepad and pen in your pocket, but I like to carry my smartphone with me so that I can record any inspiration multiple ways.

For instance, I may record a voice memo of ideas that come to me, or take some pictures of things that inspired me that I'll perhaps want to write about later.

I personally bought a Galaxy Note phone so that I can literally write notes since sometimes the act of writing longhand works wonders when it comes to getting the creative juices flowing.

The bottom line is that the tool that you use to record your thoughts doesn't really matter, but trust me, if you don't have some way to record your thoughts that come to you as you're walking, you'll likely forget the brilliant flashes of inspiration by the time you get home.

A couple of items to note here:

Your "morning" walk can occur at any time of the day. I personally like morning because then it sets the tone of the rest of the day, but if it works better for your schedule, you can walk later in the day as well.

You can also incorporate a walk with a more intentional writing time by carrying a laptop with you, walking to a nearby park, and doing some writing while there.

Writing Prompt

Write about your favorite place to walk, and how you could incorporate this into your blogging routine.

.

CHAPTER 10
CHANGE YOUR SCENERY

While blogging rituals and routines can be very powerful, if you've fallen into a rut with your blogging and you just can't seem to get into the groove with it, try changing your scenery!

For example, I usually write blog posts at my desk in my office, and while that works for me, sometimes I need to step away from my desk and do something different.

Here are some places you may want to go to write blog posts if you need a break from your normal writing location:

1. The library

The library isn't just a great place to get books and other type of media for free. It can also be a great place to study -- or write blog posts!

Most libraries have free Wi-Fi, so if you need to connect to the Internet while there, that shouldn't be a problem. That works well for me because I tend to compose my blog posts in Google docs, and depending on the frame of mind I have while at the library, may also upload my blog posts to my website so that I don't have to go back in and do it later.

Another thing I love about the library is that there are obviously plenty of resources available if I need to look something up or get some inspiration. I do have to be careful, though, not to get sucked into something like reading a magazine!

2. The nearest Starbucks or your favorite coffee shop

Let me say that I personally find Starbucks, Panera, and other similar places to be a bit distracting. I actually don't do well with noise and activity around me, so unless I'm stuck waiting around for something such as an appointment, I don't typically choose Starbucks as my writing place.

I mention it here simply because some people find it to be a great place to write, and the activity level actually helps them blog. Try it out to see if it works for you!

3. A local church

This option actually works best if you attend a church regularly, and the people there know you. :) I once attended a church that was just a block away from my local library, and every now and then when I went to the library to write, there was some type of event such as a ladies' knitting circle that made the noise level higher than what works best for me.

In those cases, I went over to the church to write, since the people there knew me and didn't mind me finding a quiet corner to write.

4. A hotel lobby

Hotel lobbies are often beautiful places, and most have free Wi-Fi, so if being surrounded by beauty inspires you to blog, give writing in a hotel lobby a shot.

I've never once been asked what I'm doing, or whether or not I'm staying in the hotel. There's generally so much activity going on in a hotel lobby, and even if the hotel staff thinks you're not staying there, they typically won't bother you, as long as what you're doing isn't bothering others.

5. A local park

I love going to a nearby park to write, because being in beautiful places inspires me, and it can be nice to get some fresh air.

The downside to blogging in a park is that you may not have any Wi-Fi available. That can be a real plus, though, if you tend to get distracted by the Internet when trying to write.

Note: If the sun glare makes it hard to see what's on your computer screen, head for the nearest shady spot. To have more flexibility in terms of the location within the park where you'll camp out, bring along a blanket or lawn chair so you won't be tied down to places in the park that have benches or picnic tables.

Writing Prompt

What are some places that you'd like to try writing? If you've written in various locations, write about your experiences with those locations and whether or not they help or hinder the writing process.

CHAPTER 11
A SAMPLE BLOGGING ROUTINE FOR BLOGGERS WITH VERY LIMITED TIME

I debated about whether or not to provide any writing routines, because in my view, a writing routine is a very personal, individualized thing, and I don't want to suggest that there is one right way to do things.

Having said that, I know that at times it can help to have things laid out, so the next two chapters are an attempt to provide two sample routines to give you an idea of how to make all of the different elements of this *Blogger's Quick Guide to Writing Rituals and Routines* come together for you.

First, I'm going to provide a writing routine for someone who has a full time job or perhaps a very busy business and writes on the side, as a way to either generate additional income, or to help grow a business.

The second routine (which you'll find in the following chapter) is for someone like me, who makes a living by creating a lot of content, and in order for the income level to be what it needs to be, a higher volume of writing needs to be done each week.

You may identify more with one or the other, or you may be somewhere in between. Again, the point of this chapter isn't to provide you with a routine that will work perfectly for you, but instead, to help you to see how you can create your very own writing routine.

Routine #1: For the Blogger with Very Limited Time to Blog

1. Start off by setting up a dedicated place to blog.

Since blogging is something that is very much a side venture for you, be realistic with where you set up your "blogging center." If you're comfortable working on a laptop, even designating a specific chair as your writing chair can be sufficient.

The main thing is to have a place to do your writing, so that when you go there, you immediately get into writing mode.

2. Determine the time of day, or a specific day of the week that you will write, and your specific writing goal for that time.

The key is to spend time writing consistently, so be realistic here and consider your other commitments when making this commitment.

For example, you may only be able to devote 30 minutes per day to writing, or two hours every Saturday. Or you may decide to use a word count goal, and make it a modest goal of writing 500 words per week, which would be equivalent to a single blog post.

3. Determine how you'll refuel your writing soul.

A couple of options that I mentioned in previous chapters

include weekly artist dates, and quarterly or annual writing retreats.

A weekly artist date may be a bit much if your time is super limited, but an artist date once a month would certainly be something to look forward to. Depending on your budget, and family and other responsibilities, determine whether or not you'll go on a quarterly or an annual writing retreat.

Now here's an example of what this would look like in specific terms for a blogger with limited time that we'll call Jack.

Jack gets up at 6:00 a.m. and after showering and getting ready for work heads to a Starbucks that is on the way to his office. After buying a cup of coffee, he finds a quiet table in the corner and writes for 30 minutes every day before going to work.

He literally sets a timer and writes as much as he can before the timer goes off. Setting the timer helps him to get out of the house on time because it indicates a commitment to write for 30 minutes, and since he wants to stay on good terms with his boss, he can't afford to be late for work.

Weekends are reserved for family, so except for an artist date that he goes on once a month, he focuses on time with family on the weekend.

Once every quarter, he heads to a friend's cabin, and spends the day planning out his blog posts for the next quarter, and getting a head start on writing some of his posts.

Even though his writing time is limited, practicing these small writing rituals and routines on a regular basis helps Jack to blog consistently, and make progress in his goal of working toward being able to quit his job to focus on his business full time

.

CHAPTER 12
A SAMPLE BLOGGING ROUTINE FOR "MEGA" WRITERS

ROUTINE #2: This routine is for the blogger who is making a full-time living creating content, or using high amounts of content to grow her business.

Here are some basic principles for the blogger/content creator who wants content to be a big part of what she does each day.

1. Decide where you're going to write

In a similar way as the very part time blogger, if you're a blogger/content creator who plans to put out massive amounts of content you'll want to decide where you're going to create content.

If you do a lot of writing, you may want to have multiple places where you create content. For example, I write a lot of my first drafts sitting in bed with my laptop, and tend to do my final drafts, where I find images and do all of my formatting and other fine tuning of my posts sitting at my desktop computer in my office.

I also spend one half day a week writing at the local library up the street from my home. Going to the library indicates I'm in "serious writing mode" and is where I push through with my bigger writing goals for the week. This is especially helpful when I am falling behind in my writing goals.

2. Block out times to write.

The difference between you as a "mega writer" and the person with very limited times to write is that your blocks of time should be bigger and/or more frequent.

For instance, my goal is to write four hours per day, and I accomplish that by writing for a solid two hours before doing any other work. Devoting the first two hours of my day to writing ensures that I keep moving forward on my goals in a very big way, so that even if I don't get my other two hours in, I've at least made some good progress and can end the day feeling good about what I've done.

You can also set a daily or weekly word count goal. While this is a good idea for the person who writes on a much smaller scale, it can be even more important for the person who plans to write two or more hours per day.

The reason this matters is that when there are big blocks of times to write, it can be easy to spend two hours in front of the computer in "pokey" mode, getting very little writing done. I'm speaking from experience here! So for those who really want to crank out the content, I recommend an approach that focuses on both time and word count.

3. Decide how you're going to refuel

As someone who is doing a higher volume of writing, you'll need to make a point of refueling more than the person who is blogging very part time, so make a point of having a weekly artist date, and being as strict about it as possible. It doesn't have to be anything fancy. Going to a local tea or coffee shop with a nice vibe and journaling does it for me!

4. Schedule your writing retreats

Finally, to help you move forward even more, set aside time for a monthly, quarterly or annual writing retreat. The big value of the retreat will be brainstorming content ideas and planning out content for the coming quarter, or if your retreat is annual, for the coming year. If you don't have the budget to get away for a retreat, try doing a "retreat" once a month at your local library, or a park or some other place where you can focus on getting a lot done in a short period of time.

Now here is a sample writing routine for a mega blogger/content creator that we'll call Janet.

Janet gets up promptly at 5:00 every morning, and after grabbing a cup of coffee, gets back in bed with her laptop, and her coffee on her bedside table.

She sets a timer for 60 minutes and writes as much as she can during that time. When the timer goes off, she goes downstairs to her kitchen and pour herself another cup of coffee, pops a bagel in the toaster, and with bagel and coffee in hand, gets back in bed with her laptop and writes for another 60 minutes.

By the end of this time, she has completed her minimum of two hours of writing for the day.

She then takes a break from her computer, as she takes her dog on a walk in a nearby park. While this time isn't writing time, she is still in writing mode since she has spent the first couple of hours of her day writing.

When she returns home, she showers, and then heads to her desk by 8:00, where she checks email to see if any of her clients need anything from her. She spends the next two hours working on client work to make sure they are well taken care of.

After a short break, it's time to polish the work that was done first thing in the morning, so she heads back to her desktop to upload blog posts she's written, find images for them, format them, and make sure they are optimized for SEO.

By this time, it's time for lunch, and since she's been very focused on writing, Janet takes a nice, long lunch break where she not only eats, but heads to the gym for some exercise.

By this point, it's early afternoon, and Janet still has some writing to do to get her final two hours in. Janet's starting to get tired, so at this time, the routine is to grab her laptop and stretch out on her couch to do another hour or two of writing before calling it a day (at least when it comes to her writing).

Her schedule is a grueling one, so she desperately looks forward to her weekly artist date, where she heads to a quaint tea shop on Main Street in her little town. She goes there to refuel, not to write, but takes her laptop or journal with her in case inspiration strikes.

Since writing at this level is rather draining, she is very intentional about going on quarterly writing retreats. Her quarterly retreats last between two and three days, with the first day focused on rest and pampering, and her final day (or days) focused on planning content for the next quarter.

CHAPTER 13
CREATING YOUR VERY OWN PERSONAL BLOGGING ROUTINE

I'm hoping that the two sample routines gave you some ideas, but I don't expect either of them to be 100% perfect for you, so I'd like to encourage you to create your very own writing routine.

Here are some ways to go about it:

1. Skim through the this book to refresh your memory about the various points in this book.

2. As you re-read this book, highlight or jot down anything that resonates with you.

3. Write up two possible routines -- one that is "in your dreams," meaning if time and money were no object, it's what you would do. I want you to have that in mind, because it's something worth working toward, and envisioning it is a great way to start down that path, even if you're not quite there yet.

Next, create a routine that you can reasonably do starting now. By reasonable, I don't mean that there won't be any challenges to it, but rather that with some tweaks to your schedule and other commitments, and with a bit of commitment, you can do it.

4. Pull out your calendar and put the items on your calendar. Even if you're like me, and have a bit looser style than doing things at a very specific time, putting them on your calendar can serve as a reminder to you of your plans and commitments, and can also help you reserve blocks of time for the things that are important to you.

One thing that I have found very helpful about putting things on the calendar is that if something else comes up for my scheduled blogging time that I really must do, I move my blogging time to another place on my calendar, rather than just blowing it off.

5. Be prepared to make adjustments. Routines are like budgets in that it's hard to get them 100% perfect the first time around. You may need to do some tweaking as you start to follow your routine. Don't consider this to be a failure, but rather part of the process.

6. Most of all, have fun! Writing is work, but it doesn't have to be drudgery, and especially if you incorporate artist dates and some retreats into the mix, you'll really have something to look forward to.

APPENDIX
BLOGGING PRODUCTIVITY TIPS FROM NOTABLE BLOGGING EXPERTS

One of the most encouraging books that I've read on the topic of blogging productivity is *Blog Wise: How to Do More with Less*, published by Problogger. It's a 30+ Page eBook and of course I can't share all of it with you here, but I wanted to share some tidbits with you to give you a feel for what the book is like, and to hopefully encourage you in your blogging journey.

If the following resonates with you, the book (which naturally goes into a lot more detail) will likely be helpful for you. If nothing else, these tips may help to turn the light bulb on for you. If even one of these tips resonates with you, it will be worth the time I took to compile them for you. :)

Now for some tips from blogging experts! (Note, these tips are by the named experts, but are NOT direct quotes, so please don't quote them! They are essentially my notes from my reading of Blog Wise that I wanted to pass on to you.)

1. Use mindmapping to come up with blog post ideas. Start with a single idea, and then mindmap it out from there to see what you come up with. ~Darren Rowse

2. Analyze what you're doing to determine if it's worthwhile. For instance, if you just spent 3 hours on Twitter, consider whether or not that time moved you closer to your goals. ~Darren Rowse

3. It's important to feel that the work that you're doing is significant in order to be motivated to do it day in and day out. ~Darren Rowse

4. Play to your strengths -- for example, know when you're most productive and blog during those times. ~Darren Rowse

5. Have clear blogging goals and do what it takes to make those things a priority. ~Darren Rowse

6. Plan ahead! Create your goals for your business, including your content goals, at least six months in advance. Then create tasks to help you meet your goals. ~Amy Porterfield

7. Sometimes old school (e.g. using pen and paper) is the way to go. Don't get caught up in using cool tools, and instead find what works for you. ~Amy Porterfield

8. Have a big vision, but know the small steps you need to accomplish the vision. For example, you can have very long term goals, but then break them down into 90 day, 30 day and even weekly goals. ~Brian Clark

9. Instead of being a Lone Ranger, consider working with others. ~Brian Clark

10. Especially when you're just starting out with blogging, consistency is key. The frequency doesn't need to be super often, but you need to determine a publishing schedule and stick with it. ~Abby Larsen

11. Carve out time every week to work on your blog posts. ~Abby Larsen

12. Don't just work harder, work smarter. Make a point of finding ways to streamline your processes. ~Abby Larsen

13. Limit the amount of time that you have for writing blog posts. Limiting your time makes you use your time more wisely and you'll get more done in less time. ~Matt Kepnes

14. Build up a stockpile of posts that have been well written and edited. The stockpile will enable you to publish content even when you don't have time to write more content. This makes it possible to work with your natural rhythms and still blog consistently. ~Matt Kepnes

15. Accept the fact that blogging is hard, and you're going to have to work through it. ~Heather Armstrong

16. The most important thing is to be consistent. ~Heather Armstrong

17. Focus on ongoing improvement. ~Heather Armstrong

18. Starting is the hardest part of blogging. This is true when you initially start your blog, but it is also true with every blog

post you write. So just start -- and then the rest of it will take care of itself. ~Jeff Goins

19. Find an enjoyable way to tackle unpleasant tasks. ~Jeff Goins

20. Productivity and happiness are inextricably linked together. ~Gretchen Rubin

21. Write only when you have something to say. If you have something to say, the writing is easy. ~Gretchen Rubin

22. Don't allow other people to define what it means to be productive. ~Leo Babauta

Again, all of these were loosely paraphrased from my reading of the book, *Blog Wise*. I hope you enjoyed them and found them helpful!

ABOUT THE AUTHOR

Rebecca Livermore has been a freelance writer since 1993. She got her start writing for print magazines, and then transitioned into writing for the web in 2006. Now she prefers to write for the web, but still writes for print magazines on occasion.

In addition to writing on her own website, she is a staff writer for *iBlog Magazine* (http://iblogmagazine.com/) and also does some private client work as well. Her impressive client list includes top experts in the blogging, social media, and content marketing industries including but not limited to:

*Amy Porterfield
*Michael Hyatt
*Pat Flynn
*Marcus Sheridan
*Chris Ducker
*Social Media Examiner
*. . . and more

If you need blog writing services, Rebecca has a small number of slots available for her **Blogging Your Voice** service (http://bloggingyourvoice.com/service.) On a very limited basis, Rebecca takes on private consulting clients. You can check her current availability at the URL, **http://professionalcontentcreation.com/coaching.**

www.ingramcontent.com/pod-product-compliance
Lightning Source LLC
Chambersburg PA
CBHW032018190326
41520CB00007B/521